Dear Dad
from you to me®

concept by Neil Coxon

© from you to me ltd 2010

Dear Dad

from you to me®

This book is for your Father's unique story.

It is for him to capture some of his life's key memories, experiences and feelings.

Ask him to complete it carefully and, if he wants to, add some photographs or images to personalize it more.

When it is finished and returned to you, this will be a record of his story . . . a story that you will treasure forever.

Dear

Here is a gift from me to you . . . for you to give to me.

When we are children we are always asking questions . . . well I now have some more for you.

Please answer them in the way that only you know how and then give the book back to me.

There might be a couple of questions that you prefer not to answer, so don't worry, just answer the others . . . I won't mind.

People say that we all have at least one book in us, and this will be yours.

The story of you and me that I will treasure forever.

Thank you,

with love

Tell me about the time and place you were born . . .

What are your **earliest** memories?

Tell me about your Mom and Dad . . .

What do you think your parents thought of you as a child?

What interesting information do you know about other people in our family?

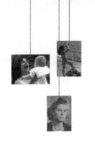

Please detail what you know of our family tree...

Here's some space for you to add more about our family that will *interest* generations to come . . .

What do you remember about the place/s you lived when you were a child?

What were your favorite childhood toys or games?

Tell me about your best friend/s as a young child . . .

What do you remember about your vacations as a child?

What kind of pets did you have when you were young and what were their names?

What were you best at when you were at school?

What did you want to do when you grew up?

Who was your best friend as a teenager... and why?

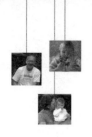

What were your favorite hobbies when you were young?

Did you have an idol when you were young?
Tell me who and why . . .

//
What was the first piece of music you bought?

What piece/s of music would you choose in your own favorite 'top 10' from when you were young?

Describe any family **traditions** you had or maybe still have . . .

What age were you when you started work?
Tell me about the jobs you have had . . .

What was the first car you owned?

Tell me about the other vehicles you have had . . .

How did you meet my Mother?

What would you do for a night-out when you were dating?

Tell me about a special piece of music that you and Mom had 'just for you'…

How long had you known my Mother when you decided to have children?

How did you feel when you found out you were going to be a father?

What did you think when you first saw me after I was born?

What were my **statistics** when I was **born**...
time of birth, weight, height etc?

What did I look like when I was born?

If you have a photo, could you stick it here please . . .

What was my nickname before I was born or when I was young?

Before I was born, what other names had you thought of calling me?

What was the first word or words you remember me saying?

Describe some of the favorite memories you have of me when I was a child . . .

What was I like when I was a child?

What attributes did I have as a child that I still have now?

What were you most proud of about me when I was at school?

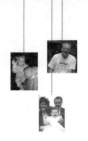

Describe what you like about me . . .

Is there anything you would like to **change** about me?

What are the happiest or greatest memories of your life?

What are a few of your favorite things?

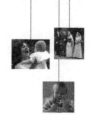

Tell me about the things that make you laugh ...

Describe your memory of some major world events that have happened in your lifetime . . .

Describe the greatest change that you have seen in your lifetime so far . . .

Describe something you still want to achieve in your life . . .

Tell me about the dreams you have for your life . . .

If you were an animal... what type of animal would you be, and why?

If you won the Lottery... what would you do with the money?

What have you found most difficult in your life?

What is your biggest regret in your life?

Can you do anything about it now?

With hindsight what would you do **differently**?

Tell me something you think I won't know about you . . .

What would you like your epitaph to say?

Is there anything you would like to say sorry for?

What piece of *advice* would you like to *offer* me?

And now your chance to write anything else you want to say to me . . .

These extra pages are for us to write any **questions, memories** or **answers** that may not have been covered elsewhere in the book . . .

And finally for the record . . .

what is your full name ?

what is your date of birth ?

what color are your eyes ?

how tall are you ?

what blood group are you ?

what was the date when you completed this story for me ?

Dear

I will treasure this book, your memories and your advice forever.

I hope you enjoyed answering my questions.

Thank you so much for doing it and for writing your own book about you and me . . .

from you to me

Dear Dad

from you to me®

First published in the UK by *from you to me*, February 2007
US version - July 2010
Copyright, *from you to me* limited 2010
Hackless House, Murhill, Bath, BA2 7FH, UK
www.fromyoutome.com
E-mail: hello@fromyoutome.com

ISBN 978-1-907048-30-2

Cover design by so design consultants, Wick, Bristol, UK
Printed and bound in the UK by CPI William Clowes, Beccles

This paper is manufactured from material sourced from forests certified according to strict environmental, social and economical standards.

If you think other questions should be included in future editions, please let us know. And please share some of the interesting answers you receive with us at the *from you to me* website to let other people read about these fascinating insights . . .

If you liked the concept of this book, please tell your family and friends and look out for others in the *from you to me* range:

Dear Mom, from you to me
Dear Grandma, from you to me
Dear Grandpa, from you to me
Dear Sister, from you to me
Dear Brother, from you to me
Dear Son, from you to me
Dear Daughter, from you to me

Dear Friend, from you to me
Digging up Memories, from you to me
Cooking up Memories, from you to me
These were the days, from you to me
Christmas Present, Christmas Past, from you to me
other relationship and memory journals available soon . . .

You can also create your own personalized version at www.fromyoutome.com

All rights reserved. No part of this publication may be reproduced, stored in a retrieval system or transmitted in any form or by any means, electronic, mechanical, photocopying or otherwise circulated without the publisher's prior consent in any form of binding or cover other than that in which it is published and without a similar condition including this.